William Willder Wheildon

New chapter in the history of the Concord fight

Groton minute-men at the North Bridge, April 19, 1775

William Willder Wheildon

New chapter in the history of the Concord fight
Groton minute-men at the North Bridge, April 19, 1775

ISBN/EAN: 9783337131494

Printed in Europe, USA, Canada, Australia, Japan

Cover: Foto ©ninafisch / pixelio.de

More available books at **www.hansebooks.com**

The North Bridge Day of Battle

OLD NORTH BRIDGE
1775.

IN THE

History of the Concord Fight:

GROTON MINUTE-MEN

At the North Bridge, April 19, 1775.

APPENDIX:

1. TOWNS ENGAGED IN THE FIGHTING AND MOVEMENTS, LOSSES, ETC.

2. MONUMENTS, MEMORIALS, ETC., ERECTED TO COMMEMORATE THE EVENTS OF THE DAY.

By WM. W. WHEILDON.

BOSTON:

LEE & SHEPARD, PUBLISHERS,

No. 10 MILK STREET.

1885.

"The Nineteenth of April, 1775: a glorious day for Lexington and Concord, for the Towns of Middlesex, for Massachusetts, for America, for freedom and the rights of man. Every blow struck for liberty among men since the 19th of April, 1775, has but echoed the guns of that eventful morning." — [*Concord Sentiment*, 1875.

"If the retreat had not been as precipitate as it was, and God knows it could not well have been more so, the ministerial troops must have surrendered, or been totally cut off." — [*Washington*.

"Before the 19th of April, 1775, I never had heard a whisper of a disposition to separate from Great Britain." — [*Jefferson*.

Speaking of the Concord Fight, Abbe Raynal says, "English blood, so often shed in Europe by English hands, irrigates America in its turn, and the civil war is commenced."

Kossuth speaks of the occurrences of the 19th April, as "the opening scene of a revolution that is destined to change the character of human governments, and the condition of the human race."

In Hayden's "Dictionary of Dates," London, 1871, 13th edition, under the head of Battles, is given the following definition: "American War: Lexington, (Gage, victor, with great loss,) 19th April, 1775."

NEW CHAPTER

History of the Concord Fight.

It is not very remarkable, perhaps, that the centennial period since the beginning of the revolutionary war should be the occasion of bringing to light some new matter in relation to its early incidents, in regard to which more or less secrecy was preserved and names withheld at the time. It seems, from evidence which has lately come to the knowledge of the writer, by a casually dropped remark concerning the Concord fight, that the alarm of the movement of General Gage to seize the cannon, stores, and ammunition in Concord, was more widely known in Middlesex County than heretofore supposed. It appears, from the testimony of Mr. Artemas Wright, of Ayer, who is a grandson of Mr. Nathan Corey, of Groton, that there were several members of the Groton company of minute men at Concord, on the morning of the 19th of April, who were in the fight at the North Bridge, and joined in the pursuit of the British troops in the retreat to Lexington.

Mr. Wright's Story.

Mr. Wright says: his grandfather repeatedly told him the story, and often talked of the scenes of that day. A part of his narration was, that on the day before the Concord fight, April 18th, while he was ploughing in his field, some distance from the middle of the town, he received notice of a meeting of the minute men, which, of course, demanded immediate attention. It was in the afternoon, toward evening, when he received the notification. He at once unhitched his plough, drove his oxen home, took down his gun and belt, told his wife Molly, as he called her, that he was going away, and could not tell when he should come back, and that she must take care of the oxen. He then hastened to the middle of the town and joined his comrades who had assembled there.

The circumstance which had induced them to call the meeting was the arrival of some brass cannon from Concord. Of course the presence of these immediately gave rise to discussion and speculation as to the cause and the reason of their being sent to Groton from Concord. Various suggestions were made, the most prominent of which was a proposition that the company should proceed at once to Concord; but this, when put to vote, was determined in the negative, most of the members preferring to wait for further intelligence.

This conclusion, it seems, was not entirely satisfactory to all the members of the company, and some of them determined to go at once; so that, as the story is related to the writer, nine of them, with young Corey among the number, started for Concord the same evening. They travelled all night, carrying lighted pine torches a part of the way, and reached Concord at an early hour in the morning, entering one side of the town some hours before the British troops entered upon the other. Mr. Corey said they all went and got some breakfast at the house of Col. Barrett, which was afterwards visited by the British troops in search of the cannon, ammunition and stores, most of which had been fortunately removed, the day before, to places of safety. After getting something to eat they proceeded toward the centre of the town, and soon joined the men of Concord, and finally were in the ranks of the minute men, at or near the North Bridge, where the fight with the British troops occurred. They continued with the minute men, and followed the retreating troops to Lexington, or beyond.

This is the story related by Mr. Wright, as often repeated to him by his grandfather Corey; and this, according to the accepted history of the time, and as at present understood, appeared to the writer, on the instant, as wholly improbable. It must still remain so unless it can be explained and accounted for in the transactions and events of the period.

The objection to be met and answered is, how could the people of Groton, thirty miles from Boston, at about the time the British troops were moving toward their boats, on the evening of the 18th, know anything of

Gen. Gage's purpose or design to visit Concord? Of course they knew nothing, excepting such information as the presence of the brass cannon, which had arrived among them, indicated. Probably the men who conveyed the cannon from Concord could not explain the matter, and yet it may possibly be true that they had learned before they left Concord, or suspected, the reason why they were sent; and, if so, would be sure to communicate it to the people of Groton. This, when we come to think of it, is not very improbable, although no reason is given in the votes of the Committee for their action. However this may be, the improbable story of Mr. Wright may possibly be explained and accounted for by the action of the Committee of Safety in the matter, by showing that the cannon were sent to Groton, and why they came to be sent there at that particular time.

EXPLANATION OF THE STORY.

Almost every person familiar with the history of this period would, on the instant, reject the story as a fiction, and nothing but entire confidence in the truthfulness of the party referred to, and the little probability there is of his being able to invent such a relation, induced the writer to give it a moment's consideration. Turning the history of the period over in our mind, the points of which were very familiar, we thought we could see a possible explanation of the matter, as a consequence of the cautionary action of Warren, and the important services rendered at this time by Paul Revere.

It is well known to most readers and students, who are familiar with the history of this period, that Dr. Warren, so far as is known by his own inclination, remained in Boston while the Provincial Congress was in session at Concord, expressly to observe the action and movements of Gen. Gage in this trying period. In consequence of some of these movements, especially that of launching the transport boats preparatory for use, and taking the Grenadiers and Light Infantry off duty, Warren determined to send notice of them, and of the preparations being made, as he believed, to capture the stores at Concord, to Hancock and Adams, then at Lexington.

This message was sent by Paul Revere, on Sunday, the 16th of April, 1775, to the effect that the British were preparing for an excursion into the country, and it was at once understood that the stores and ammunition, collected at Concord, were the object. Revere delivered his message promptly at Lexington, and returned in the afternoon, when, before going across the river from Charlestown, he made his arrangements about the signal lanterns with Col. Conant, — a matter which, no doubt, he had determined and arranged in his own mind, during his solitary ride from Lexington.

ACTION OF THE COMMITTEE OF SAFETY.

The Provincial Congress, which had been in session at Concord, adjourned on Saturday, the 15th of April, but the Committees of Safety and Supplies, who had control of the military, and other public matters pertaining thereto, did not adjourn finally on that day. They remained at Concord, and held an important meeting on Monday morning, the 17th, and, no doubt, commenced their proceedings without waiting for the arrival of Hancock from Lexington, where he had gone with Sam Adams each night during the session of Congress.

The first votes which the Committees passed, according to the record of their meetings, were as follows:

" *Voted*, that two four-pounders, now at Concord, be mounted by the Committee of Supplies, and that Col. Barrett be desired to raise an Artillery Company, to join the Army when raised, etc.; and, also, that an instructor for the use of the cannon be appointed, to be put directly in pay.

" *Voted*, unanimously, that £6, lawful money, be a Captain's pay in an Artillery Company; that the 1st and 2d Lieutenants have £4 5s.; that the Sergeants have 42s. per month, etc.

" *Voted*, that when these Committees adjourn, it be to Mr. Wetherby's, at the Black Horse, Menotomy, on Wednesday, at 10 o'clock."

After these votes were passed, it is supposed and believed, John Hancock arrived from Lexington and joined the Committee in their meeting. Of course, he immediately communicated to them the important intelligence which he had received from Dr. Warren the day before, so that, without any reconsideration of the votes just passed, any adjournment or recess, the record shows that they continued the meeting and passed the following votes:

"*Voted*, that the four six-pounders be transported to Groton, and put under the care of Col. Prescott.

"*Voted*, that two seven-inch brass mortars be transported to Acton.

"*Voted*, that the two Committees adjourn to Mr. Wetherby's, at Menotomy, [at] ten o'clock." [Not Wednesday, as first voted.]

The next day (Tuesday) a meeting was held, and it was voted that "the two brass two-pounders, and two brass three-pounders, be under the care of the Boston Company of Artillery, and of Capt. Robinson's (Company)."

[What finally was the disposition of these cannon we have no means of knowing; but, when the approach of the British troops became known, Dr. Ripley, in his "History of the Fight at Concord," says: "a considerable number of them (Concord minute men) were

2

ordered to assist the citizens who were actively engaged
in removing and secreting cannon, military stores, and
provisions. The cannon were nearly all conveyed to a
distance, some to adjacent towns, and some were buried
in the ground, and some under heaps of manure."]

Numerous other votes were passed for the removal
and secretion of ammunition, provisions, etc., and the
Committee adjourned to the next day.

On Wednesday (19th) the Committee continued its
session, at Menotomy, (West Cambridge, now Arlington,) and passed additional votes on the same subject.

Thus were the votes first passed, before the arrival of
John Hancock, rescinded, and, of course, the cannon
were not mounted, no Artillery Company was formed,
nor teacher employed for their instruction.

All this was the result of the information from Dr.
Warren, brought to Lexington by Paul Revere; to
Concord by John Hancock, and, we may almost say,
carried to Groton by the cannon! It is believed that no
other explanation can be given of the discrepancies in
these votes, so entirely different and adverse to each
other, than that which has been suggested, namely, the
arrival of Mr. Hancock after the passage of the first
named votes, and the intelligence brought by him of
Gen. Gage's movements at Boston.

SENDING THE CANNON TO GROTON.

In accordance with the final votes of the Committee, the next morning (Tuesday 18th) the cannon were promptly on their way to Groton, and arrived there late in the afternoon, while at Boston, the British troops were getting ready to embark in their boats for the opposite side of the river, on their way to Concord.

In view of what has been said, it may now be pretty confidently asked, what information did the appearance of these cannon at Groton communicate to the people, and especially the minute men of that town? It will be recollected that only a short time before this, (26th of February), Gen. Gage had sent Col. Leslie to Salem to seize some pieces of cannon there, which he failed to secure, and this was probably known to the people of Groton at this time. There cannot be a doubt, therefore, putting these two things together, as to the story the presence of these cannon told, even if the men who carried them had been speechless.

ACTION OF THE GROTON MEN.

The proceedings and action which followed, on the part of the Groton minute men, were both natural and reasonable, and fully authorized the action of the volunteers, even supposing they were moved by curiosity alone — a mere desire to see British soldiers. The

minute men, as we have stated, were promptly called
together, and some of them determined to go to Concord
that night; and, while Col. Smith was moving his troops
over the Cambridge marshes and swamps, these patriots
were on their way to meet them at Concord bridge,
without knowing who they were to meet or what was in
store for them. What followed has been stated. The
Groton minute men arrived, and were among their
brethren of Concord, Acton, Carlisle, Lincoln, and
Bedford, in following and harassing the retreating troops,
and it would seem, from the relation which we have
given, that the improbability of Mr. Wright's story has
been removed; the cannon certainly went to Groton,
and almost as certainly the Groton minute men came to
Concord. The minute men of the other towns named,
were notified of the coming of the British troops by
special messengers. The cannon sent to Acton, no
doubt, upon their arrival there on Tuesday (18th), told
the same story as did the cannon at Groton; but,
being so near to Concord, the citizens very naturally
concluded that if they were wanted word would be sent
to them at the earliest moment, as was the case; but the
Groton men, though few in number, were the first to
arrive.

Mr. Corey, who used to tell his story in relation to the
Concord fight to his grandchildren in his talk about the
war, continued in the service of his country, and prior
to his death a pension was granted to him, (or afterwards
to his widow,) but nothing was ever received by either
of them.

CONFIRMATORY EVIDENCE.

Since the first mention of this subject by the writer, Dr. Samuel A. Green, a native of Groton, has published a handsome volume, entitled " Epitaphs from the Old Burying Ground in Groton, Mass." One of the inscriptions, found upon the monument to the memory of Capt. Abram Child, contains the following sentence : " He was a Lieutenant among the minute men, and AIDED IN THE CONCORD FIGHT and the battle of Bunker Hill, 1775." The remainder of the inscription shows that Capt. Child went through the war with Washington, and was the oldest Captain in the service at the capture of Stony Point, in 1779. He was just the man for a night expedition to Concord.

Mr. George William Curtis, in speaking of this incident in the history of the Concord fight, in a letter to the writer, says : " Your new chapter throws light upon the tradition of the horseman at Acton rousing the house with the news after midnight on the 18th. The whole legend is very interesting." And, we may add, seems to be confirmed most unexpectedly from various quarters. The Groton men, of course, came down through Acton, probably after midnight, and no doubt, with or without their burning torches, produced some excitement on the road.

IMPORTANCE OF THE SERVICE OF WARREN AND REVERE.

One result of this story is particularly worthy of notice, since it shows very clearly what has scarcely ever been considered, or, in fact, alluded to, and that is the importance of the service rendered by Paul Revere in his journey to Lexington, on Sunday prior to the much more celebrated midnight ride which followed it. The story of this ride, quiet and peaceful as it was, has never been immortalized in the lines of the poet; yet it shows very clearly that the preservation of the cannon — nearly all that the colony possessed at that time — and probably the largest portion of the ammunition and stores at Concord, were saved, as we have seen, by the cautionary measures of Dr. Warren, and the essential service of Paul Revere, on the Sunday previous to the fight at Concord bridge.

Revere himself makes but very slight mention of this Sunday ride. He simply says: "The Sunday before, by desire of Dr. Warren, I had been to Lexington, to Messrs. Hancock and Adams, who were at the Rev. Mr. Clark's. I returned at night through Charlestown; there I agreed with a Col. Conant, and other gentlemen, that if the British went out by water, we would show two lanterns in the North Church Steeple, and if by land, one as a signal; for we were apprehensive it would be difficult to cross the Charles River, or get over Boston Neck." [*Revere's letter to Dr. Belknap.*]

We see now, more clearly than ever before, the importance of Paul Revere's first ride to Lexington.

NOTE.

Since this paper was read before the Bostonian Society, Mr. Wright has informed the writer that his grandfather, after he had told him the story about the Concord Fight, gave to him an old Powder-horn which he had used during the war. This powder-horn, he said, he took from a British soldier who had been shot on the retreat to Lexington, and whose body was lying by the roadside in Lincoln. Some of the other men, he said, took off his boots and some of his clothes. The powder-horn, Mr. Wright says, was quite a nice piece of work, and held just one pound of powder. It had a peculiar stopper, (probably a spring snapper, like some now known,) and at the larger end, on the under side, (when hung over the shoulder,) was engraved the English coat of arms, and on the upper side, what Mr. Wright says, they called the British Ensign. The bottom of the horn was made of brass, saucer shaped, with a hole half an inch in diameter, in the centre, serving as a tunnel, to pour in the powder, with a wooden stopper. The horn had been used by Mr. Wright and his brother, in their hunting excursions, for many years, and they agree perfectly in the description of it. It was finally lost, by the brother who owned it, in the burning of his house some years ago.

After having written the above, the writer was informed by Mr. Winsor, librarian of Harvard College, that there was a powder-horn, somewhat answering the above description, in possession of the Massachusetts Historical Society. The next day (June 11th, 1885), the writer visited the rooms of the Society, in Boston, and was shown by Dr. Green, the librarian, several old powder-horns of a similar character, all of them quite elaborately engraved and similar in many respects apparently to that described by Mr. Wright, with the exception that these all appeared to be American powder-horns, as one of them seemed to say, "To be used in the cause of liberty." Mr. Wright's story of this old powder-horn which he had, and the way his grandfather came into possession of it, and its distinct resemblance to those in use at the time, give additional weight and interest to the original story that the Groton men were in the Concord fight, on the 19th of April, 1775. The dead soldier was probably one of those buried in the Lincoln graveyard.

APPENDIX.

I. TOWNS ENGAGED IN THE EVENTS OF THE 19TH OF APRIL, 1775, WITH THE LOSSES OF EACH.

SPREAD OF THE ALARM.

Notwithstanding Gen. Gage's endeavors to keep his movement towards Concord very secret, though undoubtedly known among his officers through Lord Percy, it spread very rapidly after the troops began to move. By means of Dawes, it may have spread through Roxbury, Brookline, Brighton, Dedham, Cambridge, and Watertown: from Charlestown and from Medford, it spread very rapidly to Reading, Stoneham, Lynn, Danvers, and Salem; from Lexington, it went to Woburn, Braintree, Billerica, Newton, Weston, Framingham, Sudbury, and other towns, bringing in troops from all of them at different times during the day; from Concord, it spread in all directions, by means of the cannon and special messengers, bringing minutemen and others from all the neighboring towns at an early hour of the day.

The news of the approach of the troops was received in Concord, by young Samuel Prescott,* whose escape from the British officers on the road is well known, at about three o'clock in the morning. The alarm was immediately given to the Committee of Safety and citizens, and by the ringing of the church bell. Messen-

---

* Prescott, it is said, was afterwards engaged in privateering; was taken prisoner and carried to Halifax, where he died in jail.

3

gers were sent to Lexington and to Watertown, to obtain
further intelligence. The Lexington messenger returned
with intelligence of the firing, but did not know whether
bullets were used or not. At this time also messengers
were sent "to Hopkinton to alarm the people in that
direction; and other messengers were sent to other
towns with the intelligence; and the alarm spread like
electric fire from a thousand sources, and produced a
shock that roused all to action."

"The news," Mr. Dana says, "spread with a rapidity
almost preternatural; at noon, that day, a courier rode
into Worcester, his jaded horse falling exhausted at the
meeting-house steps, and proclaimed the tragedy at
Lexington; and the minute-men, after prayer from their
pastor, set out on their march for Cambridge." It was
expressed from Boston to Newburyport, and thence to
Portsmouth; and expresses were also sent to Newport
and Providence, thus spreading the alarm in all directions. In Connecticut, after the courier had galloped
through the State, getting a fresh horse in every town,
Gen. Hawley says: "forty-three towns started out
ninety-three companies, containing thirty-six hundred
men, for Boston." Gen. Putnam left his plough (as did
Nathan Corey,) and came to meet the enemy. "The
men of New Hampshire," it is said, "were on their way
to Concord and Lexington before night, on the 19th of
April, 1775."

It is very clear that a movement of some kind, looking
to the protection of the rights of the people, was made
in every town reached by the news during the day.
And expresses were also sent to New York and Phila-
delphia. In fact, it is almost true to say, the event
awakened the country to the true interests and rights of
the people, — and in this sense it led to the establishment
of a government, and the independence of the country.

On occasion of the Centennial Celebration, at Concord, in 1875, invitations were sent to forty-seven different towns, and adding Marlborough and Stoneham, (accidentally omitted,) makes the number forty-nine. The intention expressed was to invite those whose citizens " actually bore arms in Concord, on the 19th of April, 1775, or whose men participated in the events of the day elsewhere." The first-named class includes, —

Acton,	Chelmsford,	Littleton,
Bedford,	Concord,	Stow,
Billerica,	Groton,	Sudbury,
Carlisle,	Lincoln,	Westford,

making twelve (12) towns known to have been represented at the North Bridge or elsewhere in the town. To these were added by the Committee, as invited, —

Arlington,	Framingham,	Pepperell,
Beverly,	Lexington,	Reading,
Belmont,	Lowell,	Roxbury,
Boston,	Lynn,	Salem,
Boxborough,	Lynnfield,	Somerville,
Brookline,	Maynard,	Wakefield,
Burlington,	Medford,	Waltham,
Cambridge,	Melrose,	Watertown,
Charlestown,	Needham,	Wayland,
Danvers,	Newton,	Weston,
Dedham,	Norwood,	Winchester,
Everett,	Peabody,	Woburn,

thirty-six (36); and to these the Committee intended to add, —

Stoneham, Marlborough, Waverley (3),

making the whole number fifty-one (51). And to these are still to be added, —

Dorchester,	Malden,	East Sudbury,
Milton,	Chelsea,	and
	Harvard,	Holliston, (7)

the two first-named certainly, and the others probably, making the whole number of towns, — as at present divided and incorporated, — interested, more or less actively, in the events of the 19th of April, 1775, fifty-eight (58).

TOWNS.	Killed.	Wounded.	TOWNS.	Killed.	Wounded.
Acton, ...	3	1	Lynn, . : . .	4	2
Arlington, (Menotomy) .	3		Lynnfield, . . .	1	
Bedford, ...	2	1	Lexington, . .	10	10
Beverly, ...	1	3	Medford, . . .	2	
Billerica, ...		2	Needham, . . .	5	2
Brookline, . . .	1		Newton, . . .		1
Cambridge,*. . .	3	1	Salem, ...	1	
Charlestown, . .	2		Stow, ...		1
Chelmsford, . .		2	Sudbury, . . .	2	1
Concord, ...		5	Watertown, . .	1	
Danvers, ...	7	2	Westford, . . .		
Dedham, ...	1	1	Weston, . . .		
Framingham, . .		1	Woburn, . . .	2	3
Groton, ...			27 Towns,	51	39

In addition to the above were five missing; two from Cambridge, and one each from Danvers, Roxbury, and Lynn; but these were afterwards exchanged.

The British loss is reported as sixty-five killed, one hundred and eighty wounded, and twenty-eight prisoners, in Holmes' Annals; while an English account reports seventy-three killed, one hundred and seventy-four wounded, and twenty-six missing; total, in both cases, two hundred and seventy-three.

---

* The statement is that six of the killed belonged to Cambridge, and their names are inscribed on the monument at Cambridge. the three first named as buried there, and the three others as buried at Menotomy, (West Cambridge afterwards, and Arlington at present.) so that these latter names appear on the monument at Cambridge, and also on that at Arlington. In the above, three are given to each town.

ARLINGTON, (*Menotomy.*) "More were killed on both sides within our limits than in any other town; at least 22 of the Americans, and probably twice that number of the British fell in West Cambridge," (Menotomy.) — [S. A. Smith.] Here, Gen. Heath says, "a musket ball struck a pin out of the hair of Dr. Warren's earlock."

BEDFORD had two companies at the Concord Fight, and "they were among the eight of the foremost companies that withstood the British at the old North Bridge." The captains of both companies were killed: Capt. John Moore, at the bridge, and Capt. Jonathan Wilson, on the retreat. It was proposed, in 1879, to erect a monument to the revolutionary heroes of Bedford.

BILLERICA. Nath'l Wyman, of Billerica, was killed on the road below Brooks' tavern.

CARLISLE. At the Concord Centennial, the citizens of Carlisle carried in procession a banner, bearing the inscription, "Joseph Spaulding, of Carlisle, fired the first gun at Concord, April 19, 1775. That shot was heard round the world."

CHARLESTOWN had two persons killed at the latter end of the fighting, James Miller and Capt. Wm. Barber's son.

DANVERS. Danvers, it is said, sent a distinguished company of over a hundred men, who marched (or rather ran) sixteen miles in four hours, and suffered in the engagement more than any other company, except Capt. Parker's, at Lexington.

THE ESSEX REGIMENT, Col. T. Pickering, (740 strong,) reached Winter Hill late in the afternoon, or otherwise it might have captured the whole British force, as the men were utterly exhausted.

LINCOLN. Some of the minute-men of Lincoln (alarmed by Prescott) were out early enough to join the Concord men and march down the road before the British arrived. When the British were approaching, Eleazer Brooks, one of them, said, "Let us stand our ground; if we die, let us die here!" Capt. Wm. Smith and Lieut. Sam'l Hoar were in command.

LYNN. "How many of her sons were there, (19th of April,) she knows not to-day; she is sure of Harris Chadwell, Ephraim Breed, and Timothy Munroe, and doubts not of many more as valiant for the right as they."—[Tracy's oration, 1879.]

MALDEN. On the memorable 19th of April, 1775, Capt. Blaney's company of seventy-five men promptly marched " to resist the ministerial troops." [J. D. Green, oration on the 200th anniversary of the town, May 22, 1849.]

MARBLEHEAD men came a little too late, but they reached the line of the retreating British at or near Winter Hill, with the Essex Regiment.

NEWTON, it is said, had three organized companies of minute-men, "all of whom [218 men] were present and took part in the battles of that historic day," marching twenty-eight miles. Among them was Col. Joseph Ward, who was in Boston at the time, and hearing the news went home, "obtained a horse and gun, and rode to Concord, to animate his countrymen and get a shot at the British." On the 17th of June, he served as aid-de-camp to Gen. Artemas Ward, and rode over Charlestown Neck to execute his orders. Besides the three companies, there were 37 volunteers, "who had passed the age for military duty, and some others."

ROXBURY had 140 men in the field. Moses Whitney, Wm. Draper, and Lemuel Childs, (who kept the Peacock tavern,) had command of companies. John Greaton, (another tavern keeper,) held a commission as Colonel, dated 1774, and signed by Samuel Huntington. Gen. Warren and Gen. Heath, both of Roxbury, were on duty. One of the Roxbury companies marched four miles, (to Rev. Mr. Gordon and back,) *to attend prayers*, and lost one man in the fighting.

SUDBURY had two companies in the field, who arrived at Concord just before the British retreated from the Bridge, and joined in the pursuit down the road to Lexington. They were prominent in the fight below Brooks' tavern.

WALTHAM. In January, 1775, the inhabitants voted that they would "all be prepared and stand ready equipt as minute-men." A company commanded by Captain Daniel Whiting, "participated in the fight at Lexington." In this company, Samuel Benjamin, "grandfather of Gov. Washburn, of Maine, and the Washburn family of the West," was made first sergeant. Waltham also sent some powder to Lexington.

WATERTOWN. A very curious incident took place in Watertown, as related by a grandson of the prominent actor: a British soldier came down the road on horseback and inquired the way to Boston. Mrs. Barnard, who had been notified that the British were coming, went up to the man, seized the horse and his rider; accused him of "killing our folks," and took him a prisoner to the tavern. The town authorities kept him until he was exchanged. It turned out that he was wounded and stole a horse by the roadside to make his escape. The horse, it is said, was afterwards returned to its owner, Col. Stedman, of Cambridge, who had ridden to Lexington on him that morning.

2. Monuments, etc., Erected to Commemorate the Events of the Day.

CONCORD MONUMENT.*

The well-known Concord Monument, designed by Solomon Willard, is in the form of an obelisk, on a large square base; is twenty-five feet in height, was completed in 1836, and bears on the west side the following inscription, written by Rev. Dr. Ripley, cut upon a slab of white Italian marble :

Here,
On the 19th of April,
1775,
was made
the first forcible resistance
to British aggression.
On the opposite Bank
Stood the American Militia.
Here stood the invading Army,
And on this spot
The first of the enemy fell
In the War of that Revolution
which gave
Independence
To these United States.

In gratitude to God,
And
In the love of Freedom,
This Monument
was erected
A.D. 1836.

---

* It was proposed to lay the corner stone of this monument on the 19th of April, 1825, the semi-centennial anniversary, when Edward Everett delivered the oration; but owing to a disagreement on the question of location, the work was delayed for ten years. It was thought by many persons that the monument should be erected where the minute-men fell, and not where the British regulars fell. The erection of the Minute-man, on the opposite side of the river, in 1875, has forever settled this controversy, and it was for this purpose that Mr. Hubbard left his bequest.

THE MINUTE-MAN.

The Statue of the Minute-man first assumed shape in clay, at the hands of Mr. Daniel C. French, in 1873, and was soon after accepted by the committee and the town. Through the influence of Judge E. Rockwood Hoar, then representative in Congress, ten pieces of condemned brass cannon were granted to the town, and sent to Chicopee, Mass., where the Statue was cast from the model prepared by Mr. French. The expense of the work was partly paid from a bequest of one thousand dollars from Ebenezer Hubbard.

The Statue was placed on its pedestal, and unveiled in the Celebration of April 19th, 1875. In front, on the pedestal, are these lines from Mr. Emerson's ode:

> " By the rude bridge that arched the flood
>   Their flag to April's breeze unfurled,
> Here once the embattled farmers stood
>   And fired the shot heard 'round the world."

On the rear face of the pedestal is this inscription:

1775.
NINETEENTH
OF
APRIL,
1875.

LANDMARKS.   On occasion of the celebration of the 250th anniversary of the settlement of the town of Concord, Sept. 12, 1885, the following revolutionary memorials were erected: on the Buttrick farm, a slab in the stone wall, bearing the following inscription:

" On this field the minute-men and militia formed before marching down to the Fight at the Bridge."

On a boulder on the Boston road, over which the British went out of the town:

" MERIAM'S CORNER.   The British troops retreating from the Old North Bridge were here attacked in flank by the men of Concord and neighboring towns and driven under a hot fire to Charlestown."

CONCORD MASS.

LEXINGTON MONUMENT.

At Lexington, besides the Monument, are bronze Statues of Hancock and Adams, the former by Thomas Gould, and the latter by Martin Milmore, both modelled in Rome, and both reached Boston, (though shipped a month apart, one by steamer and the other by a sailing vessel,) on the same day, and both reached Lexington just one hundred years from the time the originals arrived there from Concord, April, 1775. There are also in the Town Hall, Statues of a Minute-man and of a Soldier of the civil war of 1861, both from the studio of J. G. Batterson, of Hartford, Conn.

INSCRIPTION ON THE MONUMENT.

"Sacred to the Liberty and the Rights of Mankind!
The Freedom and Independence of America,
Sealed and defended with the Blood of her Sons.
This monument is erected
By the inhabitants of Lexington,
Under the patronage and at the expense of
the Commonwealth of Massachusetts,
To the Memory of their Fellow Citizens,
Ensign Robert Munroe, and Messrs. Jonas Parker,
Samuel Hadley, Jonathan Harrington, Jun'r,
Isaac Muzzy, Caleb Harrington, and John Brown,
of Lexington, and Asahel Porter, of Woburn,
Who fell on this field, the First Victims to the
Sword of British Tyranny and Oppression,
On the morning of the ever memorable
Nineteenth of April, An. Dom. 1775.
The Die was cast!
The Blood of these Martyrs
In the Cause of God and their Country
Was the Cement of the Union of these States, then
Colonies, and gave the spring to the Spirit, Firmness,
And Resolution of their Fellow Citizens.
They rose as one Man to revenge their Brethren's
Blood, and at the point of the Sword, to assert and
Defend their native Rights.
They nobly dar'd to be free!
The contest was long, bloody, and affecting;
Righteous Heaven approved the solemn appeal,
Victory crowned their arms; and
The Peace, Liberty, and Independence of the United
States of America was their Glorious Reward."

LEXINGTON MEMORIAL LANDMARKS.

. The Town of Lexington has recently (1884–5) added a series of landmarks to memorable spots connected with the events of the 19th of April, in that town. These comprise three " memorial stones" to identify places of importance during the retreat; nine " memorial tablets," eight of them of wood, placed upon old houses and taverns, and one of slate indicating the spot where " the remains of those who fell in battle" are deposited; and four " principal monuments." These last comprise a monument in memory of Capt. John Parker, commander of the minute-men, over his grave; the next is a large boulder of twelve or fifteen tons, having carved upon one face a musket, powder-horn, and an inscription in the words of Capt. Parker, " Stand your ground; don't fire unless fired upon. But if they want to have war, let it begin here." The third is a monument at the south end of the Common, of Jonesboro' granite, representing a reading-desk with a closed book upon it, placed upon the site of " the first three meeting-houses built in Lexington." The inscriptions on the panels are historical, and include the names of the pastors down to 1846.* The fourth monument is in the High School yard, on the main street, and " is a unique and picturesque object," representing a large mounted cannon, carved in granite, placed on the spot where one of Earl Percy's cannon was placed in order to sweep the road.

* During the war, from 1775 to 1783, the 19th of April was observed in these churches and sermons preached as follows: 1776, by Rev. Jonas Clark, the pastor; '77, Rev. Samuel Cooke, of Cambridge; '78, Rev. Jacob Cushing, of Waltham; '79, Rev. Samuel Woodward, of Weston; '80, Rev. Isaac Morrill, of Wilmington; '81, Rev. Henry Cummings, of Billerica; '82, Rev. Phillips Payson, of Chelsea; '83, Rev. Zabdiel Adams, of Lunenburg. On this last occasion, Gov. Hancock, first Governor of the Commonwealth under the Constitution of 1780, was present, and received the honors of the occasion. The bells were rung, cannons fired, etc.

1.   Granite Boulder on the Common :

"Line of the Minute-men, April 19, 1775. Stand your ground.   Don't fire unless fired upon; but if they mean to have war, let it begin here. — *Capt. Parker*."

2.   Parker Monument in the Grave-yard :

" To the memory of Capt. John Parker, born July 13, 1729. Commander of the Minute-men, April 19, 1775.   Died Sept. 17, 1775.   The town erects this memorial, 1884."

3.   Granite Reading Desk on the Common :

"Site of the first three meeting houses in Lexington. 1. Built 1692, when the town was a parish of Cambridge. 2. Built 1713, on the incorporation of Lexington.   3. Built 1794; burned 1846. This spot is thus identified with the town's history for 150 years." [On the other side are the names of the pastors, viz: Benj. Esterbrook, John Hancock, Jonas Clarke, Avery Williams, Charles Bridges, Wm. J. Swett, Jason Whitman: 1692 to 1846.]

4.   Granite Mounted Cannon :

"Near this spot Earl Percy, with re-inforcements, planted a field piece to cover the retreat of the British troops, April 19, 1775."

1.   Memorial Stone, near Bloomfield Street :

" On the hill to the south was planted one of the British field pieces, April 19, 1775, to command the village and its approaches, and near this place several buildings were burned."

2.   Memorial Stone on the Concord Road :

"At this well, April 19, 1775, James Hayward, of Acton, met a British soldier, who raising his gun said, you are a dead man, and so are you replied Hayward.   Both fired, the soldier was instantly killed and Hayward mortally wounded."

3.   Memorial Stone near Fiske Hill :

" This bluff was used as a rallying point by the British, April 19, 1775 ; after a sharp fight they retreated to Fiske Hill, from which they were driven in great confusion."

On a Slab, near the Monument, it is said :

" The remains of those who fell in the battle of Lexington were brought here from the old cemetery, April 20, 1835, and buried within the railing in the rear of this monument."

ACTON MONUMENT.

The monument at Acton was built and dedicated October 29, 1851 ; oration by Hon. George S. Boutwell, of Groton ; poem by Rev. John Pierpont. It bears the following inscription :

"The Commonwealth of Massachusetts and the Town of Acton, co-operating to perpetuate the fame of glorious deeds of patriotism, have erected this monument in honor of

CAPT. ISAAC DAVIS,

and privates ABNER HOSMER and JAMES HAYWARD, citizen soldiers of Acton, and provincial minute-men, who fell in Concord Fight,

Nineteenth of April, A. D. 1775.

On the morning of that eventful day, the provincial officers held a council of war, near the Old North Bridge, in Concord, and as they separated, Davis exclaimed, "*I havn't a man that is afraid to go*," and immediately marched his company from the left to the right of the line, and led in this first organized attack upon the troops of George III, in that memorable war, which, by the help of God, made the thirteen colonies independent of Great Britain, and gave political being to the United States of America."

"ACTON, APRIL 19th, 1851."

On a gravestone, in Acton, is the following inscription :

" In memory of Mr. James Hayward, son of Capt. Samuel and Mrs. Mary Hayward, who was killed [and killed his opponent] in Concord Fight, Apr. 19th, 1775, aged twenty-five years and four days.

> " This monument may unborn eyes tell,
> How brave young Hayward, like a hero fell,
> When fighting for his country's liberty,
> Was slain ; and here his body now doth lye.
> He and his foe were by each other slain,
> His victim's blood, with his, the earth did stain,
> Upon the field he was with victory crowned,
> And yet must yield his breath upon that ground.
> He express'd his hope in God, before his death,
> After his foe had yielded up his breath.
> O, may his death a lasting witness *bre, (be)*
> Against oppression, and bloody cruelty."

ARLINGTON MONUMENT.

(MENOTOMY AND WEST CAMBRIDGE.)

A plain granite obelisk, nineteen feet high, in 1848, was placed over twelve of the patriots killed in Menotomy. Only three of the number belonged in the town, viz: Jason Russell, Jabez Wyman, and John Winship,— the same names appearing on the monument at Cambridge, erected in 1870. The twelve were buried in one grave, but their remains are now in a stone vault under the monument.

LANDMARKS.

These consist of five small monuments in different parts of the town. The first is in front of the Unitarian church, and consists of a granite column, four feet six inches high, two feet ten inches wide, upon a suitable base, one foot high, and bears the following inscription:

"At this spot, on April 19, 1775, the old men of Menotomy captured a convoy of eighteen soldiers with supplies on its way to join the British at Lexington." *

On the avenue above the town-house is the next, inscribed, —

"Site of the house of Jason Russell, where he and eleven others were captured, disarmed, and killed by the retreating British, on April 19, 1775."

The next is on Russell Park, fronting Mystic Street, inscribed, —

"Near this spot Samuel Whittemore, then 80 years old, killed three British soldiers, April 19, 1775. He was shot, bayoneted, beaten, and left for dead, but recovered, and lived to be 98 years of age."

The fourth stone is near the Arlington Hotel, corner of Arlington Avenue and Mystic Street, inscribed, —

"Here stood Cooper's Tavern, in which Jabez Wyman and Jason Winship were killed by the British, April 19, 1775."

The fifth stands half a mile below the centre of the town, on the avenue near Tufts' Street, inscribed, —

"The site of the Black Horse Tavern, where met the Committee of Safety, in 1775."

* Note.— "There were two wagons, one loaded with powder and ball, and the other with provisions, guarded by seventeen men and an officer, going to the army, when six of our men waylaid them, killed two, wounded two, and took the officer prisoner: the others took to the woods, and we brought off the wagons." The wagons had been delayed by the taking up of the bridge in Cambridge.

CAMBRIDGE MONUMENT.

This Monument stands in the graveyard, near Union Square, between the two prominent churches, (Episcopalian and Unitarian,) on the west side of the Common. It is a very handsome work, of dark polished marble, about ten feet in height, on a granite base, and bears on its front the following inscription :

Erected by the City
A. D. 1870,
To the memory of
John Hicks,
William Marcy,
Moses Richardson,
Buried here.
Jason Russell,
Jabez Wyman,
Jason Winship,
Buried in Menotomy.
MEN OF CAMBRIDGE.
who fell in defence of
The Liberty of the People,
April 19, 1775.
" O ! what a glorious morning is this !"

DANVERS MONUMENT.

On the 20th of April, 1835, the corner-stone of a monument to the memory of the seven young men of Danvers, who were killed at Arlington (Menotomy), on the 19th of April, 1775, was laid in that town, with interesting ceremonies and an address by Daniel P. King, Esq. The occasion was the sixtieth anniversary.

The names and ages of the young men were as follows : Samuel Cook, 33 years; Benjamin Daland, 25; George Southwick, 25; Perley Putnam, 21; Jotham Webb, 22; Henry Jacobs, 22; Ebenezer Goldthwait, 22.

" Dulce et decorum est pro patriâ mori."

PERSONAL MONUMENTS.

LINCOLN MONUMENT. This is a broad, heavy slate stone, bearing the following inscription :

" Five British soldiers, slain April 19, 1775, were buried here. Erected by the town of Lincoln, 1884."

WATERTOWN has a Granite Monument to the memory of Joseph Coolidge, the only citizen of that town that fell in the fighting of the 19th of April, 1775. It was erected in 1875.

MEDFORD has a beautiful Granite Monument " Sacred to the memory of John Brooks, who was born in Medford, in the month of May, 1752, and educated in the Town School. He took up arms for his country on the 19th of April, 1775," and served in the war ; and was Governor of the State, 1816 to 1823. Medford lost two men in the fighting.

LYNNFIELD has a Monument in memory of Mr. Daniel Townsend, who was killed at Lexington, April 19, 1775.

WESTFORD. John Robinson, of Westford, a Lieut.-Colonel in a regiment of minute-men under Col. Wm. Prescott, was a prominent man of the day ; and upon his gravestone it is said, " In 1775, he distinguished himself by commanding the corps of soldiers who first opposed the menacing attempts of the British troops at Concord Bridge."

GROTON. Monument to the memory of Capt. Abram Child, born in Waltham, and died in Groton, Jan. 3, 1834, aged 93 years. " He was a lieutenant among the minute-men, and aided in the Concord Fight." In 1779, at Stoney Point, he was the oldest captain in the service under Gen. Wayne.

CONCORD. In the old hill Burying Ground, at Concord, where it is supposed some of the British soldiers were buried, there stands a large gravestone in memory of Col. John Buttrick, who commanded the militia companies which made the first attack upon the British Troops, at Concord North Bridge, on 19th April, 1775. " Having with patriotic firmness shared in the dangers which led to American Independence, he lived to enjoy the blessings of it, and died May 19, 1791, aged 60 years."

In the same cemetery is a gravestone to the memory of Col. James Barrett, son of Benj. Barrett, who was Colonel of the regiment organized in March, 1775, and was in command on the 19th of April, though then 64 years old.

Two British soldiers, killed at the Bridge, were buried beside the wall. The grave is now enclosed by stone posts and iron chains, the work of some English citizens of Waltham, in 1875 ; and cut in the wall are the words : " Grave of British soldiers." Others were buried in the town graveyard.

WHAT IS SAID OF THE DAY.

The fight at Concord Bridge, followed as it was by a continuous warfare along the road to Charlestown, was the inauguration of the war which secured independence to the country. " Every one of the towns whose inhabitants participated in the events of the 19th of April, 1775, would have a story to tell, and would desire that the heroes of their own neighborhood should receive particular honor." "Whoever died on that day, standing in arms for his country's defence, is a sharer in the glories of the fight and the victory." — [*Concord Centennial.*]

ENGLISH ACCOUNTS.

In England, says a letter from London, "the intelligence, so contrary to the expectations of the government, * * * * has panic-struck the administration and their tory dependents."

" The rebels were monstrous numerous, and surrounded us on every side. We killed some hundred and burnt their houses."

" Lord Percy had about 1800 men on the march from Lexington to Charlestown, while beyond Lexington the enemy was less than 800, and as the Americans seemed to fall from the clouds, the numbers opposed to each other, below Lexington, was about three times those above Lexington."

When Percy's recruits went out through Roxbury, "the band played Yankee Doodle;" when they came back, one asked his brother officer, " how he liked the tune now." " D —— n them, (said he,) they made us dance it till we were tired."

" Even the people of Salem and Marblehead, above 20 miles off, had intelligence and time enough to march and meet us on our return; they met us somewhere about Menotomy, but they lost a good many for their pains." [*Diary of an unknown British officer.*]

" The troops were all the remainder of the day on their retreat to Charlestown, and many of the officers who have returned, say they never were in a hotter engagement." [*Private letter*]

Stedman says, when the retreating troops reached Lexington, "they were so much exhausted with fatigue that they were obliged to lie down for rest on the ground, their tongues hanging out of their mouths, like those of dogs after a chase." [Things were worse at Charlestown: they had all travelled from twenty to thirty miles, without rest or food. Their supply of food and ammunition had both been captured, and they had a remarkable escape from Col. Pickering's regiment.]

CONCLUSION.

After the 19th of April, the PROVINCIAL CONGRESS sent an address to the PEOPLE OF ENGLAND, in which they assure the King of their determination " not tamely to submit to the persecution and tyranny of his evil ministry:" and add, "*appealing to Heaven for the justice of our cause,* WE DETERMINE TO DIE OR BE FREE."

www.ingramcontent.com/pod-product-compliance
Lightning Source LLC
Chambersburg PA
CBHW021456090426
42739CB00009B/1753